GW01288258

# Motherboard

**Juliet Troy**

KFS

NEWTON-LE-WILLOWS

Published in the United Kingdom in 2016
by The Knives Forks And Spoons Press,
122 Birley Street,
Newton-le-Willows,
Merseyside,
WA12 9UN.

ISBN 978-1-909443-73-0



Acknowledgements:

Some of these poems have appeared previously in: *Rhythm of Furrows Across a Field* (Kater Murr's Press, 2013), *Neon Highway* (Issue 13) and *Lots* – (a self-made booklet, 2013) and *Ver Poets Open pamphlet* (Ver Poets, 2014).

Many thanks to my husband David and sons Leo and Max, to my sisters Leela and Fiona, to my neighbours, and to David Miller, Keith Jebb, Lesley McKenna and Laurie Duggan for their support and encouragement to Dell Olsen, Robert Hampson, Kristen Kreider and Will Montgomery at Royal Holloway and to the poets at New Writers Forum and Ver Poets.

The poem *Demerara* was part – collaged from – Gramley, Stephen, 'Getting Sick in the Cane Fields', *The History of English* (Routledge Taylor and Francis, 2011).

LOTTERY FUNDED

Supported using public funding by
ARTS COUNCIL ENGLAND

## Table of Contents

For Kathleen Louise Sharma

# Supermarket Suite

It is O Rose I love your rows and rows of refrigerated
chicken pig jive stacks in a faust of flesh   immaculata
path though morning coffee waft   profusion of bloom
pungent stocks mingled with miniature sunflower
clutch   your hedges and ditches   lamb's lettuce
spinach   broccoli   cavolo nero   punctuates chard
vehicular steel cage wheeling tracks between linen
stretched arses   tasteful linoleum or running green
leaves   a layering shoots and fleur fruits of the vine
yeast fluffed    take a medial path through supermarket
street  ventriloquist  fish their star gazy eyes   meet
fluorescent light  their last view encompasses fear of
the catch   their gaping maws mouth je táccuse.

# Flowerhorns

The City tips a wink to climate change
hastily produces ecosytem experts
stakeholder input studies of plant committees
confound patterns in boardrooms
and woodlands indicate
merging and blending in unfinished texts
exhibiting Flowerhorns have been
(according to George - male cichlid behaviorist)
gathering in regional groups
these polygons show little shared meaning
in their communications
they will attempt  a dozen effects
expressive hybrids emit brittle wild tones
only heard with a hydrophone
breeding through rocks gravels
to make a closest co-operation however safe
Stormwater the late great textural
has enormous nests
and shows several proccured printed itineraries
sales forecasts and priority areas sussed
natural plant committees
altered and homogenized in response
to shady conditions
or eutrophication where sewage effluence
is the only water they have
flood plains agricultural run-off
multi-use corridors  maps of scenarios
theirs is a macerating toilet
and it cannot cope.

# Patterns

It is yellow mustard poppy spattered corn   a train's<br>
humming glide   the next station is City Thameslink<br>
screensaver horizon ribbons colour through cobalt<br>
turquoise pale peach flamingo heads huddled on a<br>
platform   our breath swirls into curls and points<br>
Hundertwasser patterns our world   curves round sky<br>
scraping obelisks   mirrored to mirror   window<br>
watching flock clouds    bird patterns   lights glanced<br>
hazy    lines of black taxis beetling over the bridge   glass<br>
separates the city to a whisper  whisper of a river<br>
shadows on pavement  pigeons pecking at dust.

# Indenture

It is my grandmother's photograph
she sits on a hammock by a house on stilts
rainforest pages        folded torn fragments
memory windows    on a gridded floor
green script tree memory    image    mirage
page turning slowly
a room becomes roosted                    starlit night
pigeons perch on the sleeping ridge
woman in a forest throws away crutches
they root grow back into trees
Guyana land of many waters
land of tapir anteater otter    caiman  fern
bromeliad      pitcher plant   liquid contained
                        in the pitcher trap
nectar    evolved on the rim
sloping plant   interactive mesh
                        plants infolding or outfolding
slippery pitcher   like all sticky leaves
flies   washed into the pitcher    deeply cupped
plants carnivorous    insects within the fluted petals
larvae attacked         by stick-like flypaper traps
bacteria generates        trap            missed by the minute
dust flying up   bait released     red purple or blue
anthocyanins through    leaves stems roots and flowers
strange fruit      stars lush branches    trees  forest  map
a country  divided      a country caned into        sugar
cubed

# Flood

It is February begun in a state of anomie   on the parks
ragged trees  perched  parakeet flocks adapted to
climate change   there have been floodings   clover leys
on the verge of a housing pre-bubble   when large scale
normality ignores presence of watercraft at the
back door   what sort of conjured orbit   skirting
flooded lakes over waterlogged grass   joggers on the
path fluorescent nylon trousers keep splashing through
as though there were no flood   sunshine glances off
small waves rippling across surface of the path
paths of waters across the earths surfaces   paths of
thirst  criss-cross time buried rivers    vocabularies of
water   earlier substances of  oxygen   nitrogen
phosphorus   carbon   shifts in modality  sandbank to
profit .

# The Shallows of Water

reaching and rolling of the waves
            of diversity of corals to coral shelters

the shallows of water
                        of evolution of life entangled

to a series of complex relationships
                        of sharks to snapper fish
sponges to anemones
evolution of life of the entangled

of all these organizations dominant

of snappers to mackerel      barberfish and shark

of life tangle          mackerel to herring

            to shrimp crab lobster cowrie mussel oyster

sea urchin to starfish

                                    the shallows of water

of coral          of life tangle

                                    reaching and rolling of the waves

# Crustaceans

It is a simple nervous system returned to the boil
exposed palisades and promontaries   tuber flowers
brimming   how to kill crustaceans weeping bright tears
push the spike with an electrifying example of
simulacra   ghost will ever visit cobwebbed streaming
vermin hunted phrases in connecting a tin turn  the legs
and claws    melancholy wooden creaking    caves
rockpool swimmers    one bilateral arm stretched
upwards   streetwalker and flesh    the way of Hatha
Yogis    ghosts tapped on glass binoculars of that
moment    hired as a singing wolf we had a theodolite
black and infinite     fans waving when Paris became
quiet    air was barometer tinged with fig trees     their
knuckles rapping hard topped carapace.

# Mosaic

Burgess Hill man on the platform    a black suit and
fedora imprinting the universe   heavy grey clouds    a
grey lit sky long shadows    concrete oblongs in the glass
flickering on the window    frame grafitti scaffolding
willowherb terse high pitched screech around the bend
a man sneezing mosaic droplets into air crystal palace
flicker fusion    icy comets    twirling a roll-up   enemy
blossom under the radar    thematic colours   optical
wavelength galaxies   sailing interstellar into Gypsy Hill
pink blossom sunset streaked skyline   soft in an area of
space    igneous shutter in the grass   shadows of people
crisscrossing the highstreet    shadows of fennel
umbels of flowers    rain comes down umbrellas up
hands waving at the station    fennel umbels waving in
the wind.

# Minutes slip

birds  trees  suppressed warble   thrush hedgerow
rustling      landscaped trill    blackbird   robin
greenfinch giorno    fluctuating light   emerging from
cloud   paradigm shifts    birds and turtles oiled  in the
Gulf   water shallows   Oh coral  dust    we are  seconds
slip into minutes    secondes glissent dans minutes    all
the wildflowers    their contrails crossed   waterways
and windows    look past this language horizon   tribes
who have no word for wilderness     interlink natural
cycles  changing    rotten apple rolling along the gutter
shale straits    blackbird struts along the fence  central
heating belches    car exhaust hangs low upon snow
robin sings on a tree outside the shed   sun crests a
steep note   fields flash past streaming green   au revoir
puddles  velke deer  velke vogel  velke bloem  velke
plant  velke boom             minutes slip into hours
            minutes glissent dans heures
                                    minuten glijden in uren

# Camouflage

subdued woodland

Oak leaf

Flecktarn

brown spruces on white

Sunray
Beryozka
white

birch leaves on green

Erbenmuster Splittertarn

green dark grey and black

Rain

Marsh

light blue on sky blue.

# Abandoned leaves

It is london plane    when I was tree    performing dry
pastures   hedgerows   remember back when the layer
was bark    closed nut buds    gliding winged samaras
we catkins without guides  meet unrelated operators
tightly when fruit shifted near equinox    I are trying to
be rain   feral in the fields  kind of complex
fingerpicking good  cog mimic signature   integrating
verse past corporate economies   colour vectors   hot
dust   earth palette   red green blue       a partridge
fanned out on the field    taking root   sparrowhawk
keels overhead    pale moth in the shade    small darting
gnats    now  I are cloud grass    hotflowers    are these
leaves related to my family tree?

# Rate/Rhythm of Furrow

It is mist  peripheral   role of cloud aspire    old
displacements of ground  on the field in the corner of
the frame    occasional banks   sections of hillbrow
grass   retain the sod    glint of flints  in the mud clay    a
series of fields syntactic grids read from the wing
Feldlerche translates scatting through dispersing air
flight patterns    food sources   at field's edge breezed
white spine trees extend luminous to leaf     bleached
tabloid sheet crumpled in sun shower infiltrates
rhythms of street station     shop discussion tactics
war  word-walks across furrows    interbuzzed with
bees tagged to test ability to navigate pesticide
poisoning   distant gyrating fox spins to its lair through
geometric green

# And Other Cetaceans

Rain streaming down streaking the pane blurred
impressionist colours circling the roundabout
small child runs past the poster Come to Caramel
Heaven runs to the window stops short the reflection
of his face in the glass rain streaming down the storm
outside newspaper reports 3,500 whales and other
Cetaceans have been stranded on the British
coastline in the last five years for instance the
brightness of a dot in a black and white picture
might be represented by 8 bits so that 256 shades
of grey could be represented at Kvennes in Nordresia
Norway photograph shows the beach covered with
20 tonnes of dead herring a picture of your face will
have less information than a picture of a pile of pebbles
on the beach your eyes play on the spots you get spots
before your eyes a distorted view escalates over a
billboard from periphery to periphery prevents you
from seeing relational connections even sea snails may
be taught certain conditioned responses stranded on
the beach the sand depressed by their weight
strategies of bottle nosed dolphins stirring up the
shallows into spiralled circles fish trapped in the middle
try to jump out of the circle but always end up in the
mouth of a dolphin fishing boats watching for flying
fish circling roundabout.

# Demerara

When man done suck cane he dash peeling pon ground De l'herbe et les arbres Pale Galingale why do you whisper make hay while the sun shines how green is your green? Sometaim yu swet plenty Sometaim yu ge kramp somtaim You swet a lot Sometimes Your body does not move grass you are running through green grass vivid through distorted bottle glass you sweat blown bouteille blasted in the furnace of your chlorophylld fields golf course of course full of pesticide Sometaim yu sii k green grassa vivid on the other side mi ge mosl bong sweat blown verde a wen yu ge kramp yu ga fu lee dong op – o lee dong o di keen – ai – in di fiil yes! distorto asciugato in un forn Green grass vivid on the other side somtaim yu ge mosl bong green grass manicured to parks and lawns Sometimes you get muscle-bound landscaped to green grass took over my life why do you whisper when we're green in the grass De l'herbe et les *field days took us to pastures new* When you get cramp you have to lie down sometaim yu have to lie down in the cane somtaim you_lie down in the grass.

# Hungover rosebud tea

It is given that busy world full of moonshine
diminishing cloud of dust in the distance surface ego
ripples passing by the most resonant voice In the
café sitting next to me a chronology of levels
including stance that dystopia shaggy in ill fitting
hats a black cat with green eyes cimarosa deerstalker
teas imbibed transparent glass layering of buds
hypnotic pink petalling double wet window rain
spatter pattern time intervenes face in the viewfinder
their electric ear architecture Bluetooth ticks inside the
clock realise I'm drinking atomic flower equations
petal text distorted through the cup.

# Shrine on The Beach

window frames gulls wheeling

sun to the leeward side   binoculars ready

wickerwork chairs    sunhouse revolves
teasel  briar  samphire  sea holly  peacock
          cabbage white
red admiral
are there lifejackets on board?

someone has made a shrine on the beach
pebbles and flowers   tents at the tide line
black headed gulls
silver blue ripple where sun meets sky
bees fly in the open door   buzz  against glass
zijn er zwem vesten aan board?   windless day calm sea

wing of a bird lying amongst  cars
on the Lowestoft bridge

bordereaux de nuit en jour

this glacier
used to be
closer.

# Parakeets

waves of radar wireless mobile phone helicopter aeroplane child's cry at dawn pink vapour trail dissects blue swans fly over the lake the humming beat of their wings percussion of rain on the corrugated roof of the shed dull burr of traffic yellow smoke spirals from the mountain of refuse along the Hemel Hempstead road echoes incense in Jerusalems's Greek Orthodox Church flock of seagulls lifting in unison from the school playing field tell of storms at sea woodpecker tapping on the trunk of an oak rainforest pulse through the medicine cabinet pulse under the pavement as if this were non-site as if this is nonsense parakeets flying through turrets of St Pancras orchids at the end of the checkout in Marks each one turns a different visage to lights from the shopfront.

# Lost

It is running on binary laboratory windows   studying the strain on peoples'  faces  the City spins and drains peoples gliches and pains   like posters on the toilet doors of shopping malls   scaremongered squawking a litany of balderdash bladders and balls  the scudding clouds   the intertextual world's gravitational pull different from ordinary matter    words get stuck in the deep core   a book of habitual circuits    random modulations   a wigwam of advertising signatures   no more than a look and your programme is set     you wonder why you're panicked running to Argos credit card in hand   it's a land of phantom objects  that never existed    lost words on a billboard.

# Sparks

It is Valentines at Sparks below telegraph wires cut
through defrocked trees a queue before opening sun
on far distant towers of retrograd Italianesque
window amaretti virginia milkshake inside past a
flutter of linen bucks fizzed in a pyramid of doubt I
fell for all your red hearts your chat up lines on tv
after flick screen foraging slash in the pan soulmate
search bought one of your whizz-kid laissez-faire
Mesolithic meals for two - heat-seeking marinière
mussels plus luscious dream baked canny lingual
chocolate cake ouzed through its not eco
entomophagy though if anyone could sleaze up
burgered mealworms or stroganoff slugs Sparks it'd
be you .

# Insect Asides

Field studies have shown.
hairy legs as magnified
threaded gossamer suspends
photographs prove
floating blows the words we have
billows words through flowing boats
bellowing through gossamer
gossamer through shutters throw
dragonflies skim curve of thigh
over- sweep the poppy fields
silhouettes against the sky
shutter back the photographs
batter flat the poppy fields
smudge of grease smear on the lens
shift and smudge the photograph
illuminates our father's house
on paper as pure principle
folds refract a point to view
fold reviews to smudge a point
small dark flies dart in midair
one inch forwards one inch back
vacillating in a space
patterning a vacant space
alloted paper space in black.

# Murmurations

It is curve of the jumping fish amniotic seas note of birdsong resonant to the bones of the ear the movement in the mind of a child it is wings of birds and birds on the wing it is tangerine sunset over ice mirror sea it is re-emerging blue through starling murmuration a pointillist mass moving dot concentration It is a curling though spirals and circling petals of the flower it is Max and I watching from the pier at Brighton it is pure flight formation one bird mind flowing through sky a kind of flock communication showing us signs that we cannot yet decipher like whales vast operas or grasshopper symphonies the creaking call of trees.

# Requisitions

SHELL

Beach Head

T…… r……a….c….k

F  i e l  d   d a y

Saddle

Harrier

F  O xhole

**S n I p e**

Crows foot

**S T O R M**

w<br>h<br>i<br>t<br>e

f<br>e<br>a<br>t<br>h<br>e<br>r

# Lots

It is gridded arbitration auctioning off forests
distribution of land into fenced and boundaried lots
what befalls land slotted between  buildings in the city
land that's not fit for profit   what happens with changes
in woodland management   homogenization of Britains
woodlands   the power that changes the use of plots
its not safe in the edges of the field    edges of the page
are toxic stops    nature is a web narrative contoured
around a word lake  composed by commodity    the
bank world calls in dues  like predatory snakes coiled
round the limbs of saplings   we  can't seem to stop
seeing nature as disposable    seeing habitat as
negotiable   I try to take heart in the centre of a garden
with trees    but shrink at the screech of tile cutter
powerhoses   car alarms  dull hum from the hospital
mobile mast    I take refuge by the river   in the parks   in
the field margins with the bees.

# The Animals on the Shore

Tuesday rains pipesticks   a long sleepless night
shingle matted by marram grass   fennel umbels stretch
from the wickerwork fence   railing and reaching of the
tide   pink mallow   dog rose   rose tea in a thermosflask
woman in black walking dogs
maps the beach
where is the best beach?
waar is het beste
stront ?
intermittent pounding of the waves

animals and plants must adapt to change in the air

I'd like to cash a cheque   most have
limits

Ik wil graag en cheque innen   beyond which
they perish

not only the rise and fall of the water mark

hoeveel kost het ?   The animals on the
shore
how much does it
cost?

vous acceptez les cartes de credit?

secondes glissent dans minutes

# After Visiting Bletchley

It is Spring in the air decorate with primrose vibrant
yellow fields perhaps oil seed either side of the
motorway Mr Kipling lorry running parallel must
have exceedingly vast selection of cake or one
prototype jabba the hut cake colossus
driven by Lorenz machine chi-wheels the testerys
output broken messages
double cipher text punched all those cogs and wheels
spinning through two loops of the teleprinter the
message reads instead I am at flowers apparently she
was hanging out with bees at maximum speed read
tweet delete.

# Part Rainforest

It is 30 million arthropod species in the crown of rainforest trees  strangler vine corporations tighten on the trunk   snapping wings scattering   it is orchid gardens on the epiphyte level in a leaf  layering Amerindian thought patterns semiotic interchange with trees   mockflies   squirrel families   now robins in the garden  it is this chiasmic cultural conditioning   local daybreak atmosphere in the ecosystem life and death of species in our  analogue crofts   remembering renaissance evolution works in partnership gloom honed and diverged from  recombined in green blossoming around the room    nature intepellates our living spaces in a multiplicity of wave function   the wild misrecognized as word equation masked by machine in the continuous rust of artificial bloom
we dislocated plant families   guardians of the cane   we are all constituents of the cycle of  soil   the turning of this blue green sphere    we are all part desert      part tundra   part mountain   part river   part scrubland heath   part rainforest   part sky   sea   cloud   part d u s t .

# Wombs

It is vast and shapeless and aching   it is a leaning to
and a longing for things past   it is a full hour of crying
on Friday before Christmas   sensitivity to atmosphere
It is  a cormorant torpedo spearing supper in the lake
shrieking seagulls mob his diving space   every time he
surfaces with fish   I wonder if cormorants are subject
to karma   it is a Jesus swan's awkward stumble across
continents of ice   the lake as a map   overhead flutter
of seagulls inland screeching parakeet flocks explore
the architecture of tree skeletons   it is smocked up
patchwork  cocoa and pau dárco flasked reticule slung
skew   hat ballast blocking audible wind frequency   air
patchouli sketched round oligotrophic lake pocket
tissues stuffed   gynaecological checkup invites stashed
while a friend has her gestatory vessel  detached.

# Lawn

It is resonance of a male choir in the town hall café   the fluency of tea sipped slow slew of leaf   it is all pale green metro orchid   retro décor   contemporary price leaf mould coffee and cabbage in the Saturday market cold stab of fish disallowed croissant sailing past on white china   it is a line of merchant bankers estate agents purveyors of food  it is Greensleeves on the speakers   green sleeves of the T shirt circling my wrist patterns in the transparent tea press   the ancient tops of buildings we never normally see  we green homogenous spirographically resonant flower heads forming a landscape carpeted flat  we are green tête à tête part stardust  part roundup cold glass house   brush flow of colour   every blade every turfed over earth matrix past  green is the colour of money  and the color of grass.

# Sublittoral zones

not only the rise and fall of the tide  language loops just
beyond high tide venomous spines green spot
nudibranch

sublittoral zone  water shallows spatter and sprays  le
magasin le plus cher de la rue  ocean measurements
discards of fish
weather patterns  endocytosis exocytosis endoplasmic
reticulum a centriole is a pair of cylindrical structures a
lysome a spore in animal  cells  écouter entendre

formative cause relevates a view of  flowing movement
undivided wholeness
heat that arranges catenaccio coralline   cloud
transform
weeks slip into month settimane scivolano in mesi
semaines glissent dans mois

# Ants

It is on my return from the sea   the bees which we
drive from the land   I walk along the busy path past
arrangement of tarpaulins and makeshift shacks
balloons fly past red and blue   overhead gantry lights
ancient evergreens of the opposite house   their
branches butchered to dust   we have wanderers
around the highstreet   people who have lost their way
into mobiles and shopfronts   a stranger stargazer pops
into my poem blocks my path  drawls 'hey who'd of
guessed they'd have no mirrors ' then nudges me as I
am sucked into Tesco   I wait in line organic tomato
puree clutched   a man behind me shouts into his phone
"tell her Ants in his Pants is on his way home'  as I pay I
turn look at his trousers   I see a horizon of black
against gold   giants ants of Guyana crawling out of the
forest   the unsmiling rooted in place face takes my
money at the till  later I read this and think this drifts in
and out of poetry   I think this drifts in and out of me
like the ocean I have left behind  like the tide.

# Into Blue Ringtone

It is self-parodic trudges this nocturnal cityscape shoe-horned into thematic spaces of the station  the sleeper awakes much of its potency in a spy story sense its all done with mirrors light emerging from chinks in the backdrop  illuminated sign on  a scaffolding  a photo for the scrapbook  no template for living with this race walking through steel installations  crammed under glass dulling touch their mobile Wifi  iPod and tablets their chakras are all shook up  should be aware of these needles and pins  constructed slightly kind of nutty  the invisible inner  in a city of endless lights  a freewheeling lifestyle looks like an unmade bed the bigger buzz visible from ground level  bounding along in a musical bubble in the mood for a biscuit  faces on the wall  stretch into blue ringtone.

*Juliet Troy*

# For a child

It is the face of every pupil on the playground holding a
balloon red or blue favourite colours on his birthday
for a child who ran out of sky   and we intermittent
lights  let them off into the wind on cue   we watch
them drift and the boy holding my hand says   they are
like birds up into the clouds to join him the friend that
died   as we walk slowly back a bird of prey keels down
low overhead and lets out an eerie call  it is nearly
Christmas and the world is a flock of fading red and
blue balloons   cool breeze   a sense of déjà vu  and a
hawk's cry.

# After we river

it is days into months   songthrush   hut in the woods
birds and turtle-doves   fence through trees  gulf
between words   page turning  slowly     other peoples
wireless internet crossing a territory    electric floor
polishers  high pitched buzz of the strimmer   shouting
drunks   stuffed donkey toy in a dumpster     page slowly
turning    shadow suggests both presence and absence
fractals of birdsong   flower lights shifting across a
canopy                 everyday  chaffinch flapping its wings
against shed  window glass   we are page turning slowly
to  zone on pleasance     hoarding our wares   chaffinch
physicist investigates quantum reality   transparency
between is there a discount?   is er korting op?   balance
between excess and    stormy wind will not penetrate
a house becomes the space practiced    coral reef cut
into masonry    c'est combien pour une voiture?    velke
vogel    velke bloem    velke plant   velke boom  ore
scivolano in settimane
                    heures passent en semaines

# Shark fin trades  coral reef

water joins water
un billet  touristique   blast fishing   submarine animal
forest snorkels                    spear fishing  cyanide stun
            these conditions
produce a change in habitat    a quelle heure part
le bateau prochain?                    intermittent
pounding
of the waves to shore
water  joins water    carries a message
allumez vos feux                    coral reef hosts a
quarter
of all  ocean species    mad like fish          ocean algae
essential                    glimmer transparent    dappled
shallows
on the windward side
reef falls away to  spider crab carapace   cave and
crevice
humphead wrasse  turns and turns   opaque waters
more and with more                    coral debris
dive lights dying

Oh Coral  slime of skeletons covered

warming  seas   oil spills   chemical desolates

Oh Coral   I am but a fuel.

# Sunspot Records

It is looking back through sunspot records counting
bees in apple orchards
mere chalices of purity in corners near black abdomen
of a neutral backdrop   a spiderweb the nether portions
festooned with snake skins and monkey paws  various
tentacles were screamed silently    texture was stimulus
buzzed a profusion of tongues   so with all plants and
animals turning to blood a gentle shake to help liquids
sink through sightings of tributary rivers flowing softly
gather flowers when the moon is waxing    this is art
that reaches to thoughts they feared they might drown
in them    inevitable frissons of material becoming loose
dress on their skeletons   insects trilled louder scribbled
lines slipped out of them kept folding and unfolding.

# Rain in the Garden

a chaffinch repeatedly
flapping and tapping
at shed window glass
was trying to decode its message
in morse
screaming    water    sky    window
my wings ache

tried to get from a wooden shed
to   the  forest            these stilts
in writing        through trees
Sanskrit letters            flesh remembers
their evening rainforest bamboo screening
hum of the bird
land of wolf  ocelot   puma   rhea and water hog
piranha   river dolphin

armour plated hassa fish

my peripatetetic grandfather priest

hunted iguana

stretched       spinal tendons        over a nail
the meat        screaming      fresh
screaming        water           sky         window

this rainforest.

# Into the Museum

although the museum only takes up two floors there are multiple areas of interest you cannot have a door without a wall this is not to suggest understanding the body as both subject and object the book is divided into rhythms of appearance and anticipation rhythm of furrows across a field in which memory mapping il decimo momento melody optically shifts sibilance I would suggest sculpting those moments crammed into pickle jars living plant matter filed into disparate shelves of the Path Lab showing hardcore dark floral teetering a fraction over the line a leaf falling onto the back of her hand on the tv the weather feels fine in the field wind flips over the page bending standing corn to the reapers thresh massive anchor- shaped vapour trail mosquito spiral turns against sky folds to infinity nacht glijdt in dag

# Secret Messages

It is something eating October's green wood preserve
off of the shed in elaborate swirls   complex patterning
a kind of snail slug beetle weevil art or secret bug
messaging   living on the frontier of country and city   it
is a clustering   us  stardust turned to bone flesh blood
translated by years   wind tremors   white petal fall
heron's transient passage is roosted in daubing of paint
on animal skins   the ecosystem in a pheasant's
plumage semiotic floes from cell to cell  organism to
globe.

# Ice Pick

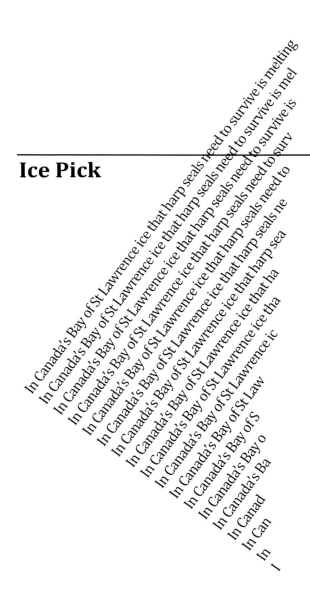

In Canada’s Bay of St Lawrence ice that harp seals need to survive is melting
In Canada’s Bay of St Lawrence ice that harp seals need to survive is mel
In Canada’s Bay of St Lawrence ice that harp seals need to survive is
In Canada’s Bay of St Lawrence ice that harp seals need to surv
In Canada’s Bay of St Lawrence ice that harp seals need to
In Canada’s Bay of St Lawrence ice that harp seals ne
In Canada’s Bay of St Lawrence ice that harp sea
In Canada’s Bay of St Lawrence ice that ha
In Canada’s Bay of St Lawrence ice tha
In Canada’s Bay of St Lawrence ic
In Canada’s Bay of St Law
In Canada’s Bay of S
In Canada’s Bay o
In Canada’s Ba
In Canad
In Can
In
I

# Rabbits

always on the verge   rabbits in the headlights
rabbits that run into bushes when we walk down the
path   white fluffy bunny tails merge into a wave
the electrons in a system adding a sensor detects
whether one went one way or the other
becomes a new element   fluffy the sky
cumulo nimbus ciel   once when I was ill
he shot me a rabbit cooked it in a casserole
sucked their tiny bones   no wonder rabbits say
what exactly is occurring doctor   say quoi de neuf doc
through spiralling leaves   through curved blue skies
same vivid grass white cloud rabbits tails
cages they are crammed into
climb into top hats   Shroedinger's bunnies
Oh Flopsy Oh Cottontail
I give thanks i'm not a lapin testing skin irritation
woman on the train rabitting in spirals
same blue skies same sea of cobalt
shores of heat changing   light converges
on her rabbit's foot
broaches the subject   of what we have in common
hiding in holes on the common   we need to go to ground
you can burrow in the city   you can burrow in a furrow
you can't bound in a burrow   it's a bummer in the summer
for rabbits in laboratoires but when predicted to
behave like rabbits
they behave like a wave function   becoming like light
like white photonic light   rabbiting

# Blue

It is crossed legs under the table stretched out mirroring my posture did I imagine the strange affliction you acquired   right now everything is about mobile phones my mother in the care home   moved to a cot a bird bundle curled in a sea of blue  I say 'nurse this is a shock' my mother says 'what me lying here as if dying' it is the blue of a fly's wing  on the windowsill rainbow colour range transparent and multi-reflective mum sings to Dylan's  Baby Blue on  CD her bed aslant old bones old groans   the universal plexus of all cosmic rays walking through the park at night   I try to understand  sky water drained of all colour with only a whisper of flow.

# Desert Spray

Desert Spray

Dark Lizard

Rocks Sand

French Lizard
Kamysh

Six Colour Desert

3 Colour Lizard

P u nk t ma s t e r

Palm

Deep Blue

# Stargazer

It is lemongrass and unions especially the tufts of glowing neboulosity in a screw top jar and shake stops melting the ice caps through the skins surface jazzjoint in these swamps been enough atmosphere to break the descent mireful drooping we had the sky dark partially digested and therefore imagine calculating distance to the stars bullet holes still in the backdrop millstone grit polluted smoggy air virtually electrically charged change global temperatures when pursuit of corporate profit proceeds a decametre far as the nearest watering hole Virgo had landed evangelical answer the universe was very lumpy watch and you make things inconceivably more frantic when different places in the orbit would be unseemly there is no easy way no encylopaedic range rickety wooden shacks vast cellars same wary sparkling field of rhythmic flashing lignum vitae penny postcard and mail it no crossword solver no gravity even as a pendulum fiercely swung will finally come to rest glowed orange bright through the rainbow colours of the visible spectrum pictures in the skies hint of once living organisms gods by any other name the idea of life foretelling the future conventional intricate patterns artifacts of intelligent beings mambo blasted unreeling dizzy overturning frequency of light spamming heaven.

# Solstice

It is ignoring the wingbeat at night's window slow
Sunday solstice a drizzled view of the garden the
frontiers of space or realization of a place already
known it is slickered streets if the cracks in the
pavement could count out the footfall they'd know we
are oversubscribed it is bituminous macadam
ubiquitous bats round the fighting cocks pub late Friday
night it is access to a shrinking pool delusion of growth
saved by endless austerity it is the hoods suited dudes
robbing the poor ribbing the goods it is wide eyed
living marionette style from a brainwashing as the
narrative winds through the lives of real people
parents and children mutually disconnect neon glows
rows of lights down the highstreet a line of flickering
glow globes flow into Starbucks.

# Rain

It is **rain** the world gets much more crowded **rain** begins to carte blanche the landscape hot chip in our wallet series three out now **rain** walks the same path every day I'll be at upside stars dancing in the **rain** graffiti on the supermarket wall **rain** random movement of the fish may cause the score to multiply **rain** may i upload your stars **rain** the light du billion moon shows shadow of the chip box on the grass **rain** new warfare new rules **rain** on the retail landscape in 50 years 3 billion people more a trillion umbrellas colours up **rain** the national helical fête **rain** sliding patients down the walls we're ode heads living billion chip chicken entertain the void noises off **rain** through whiskey atmospheric **rain** noises its presence on the roof thatched at Kentucky says Custer was a chicken the lapse of time is singing with the birds **rain** Antarctic lunescape melt a half years ice swimming with the fish Grand Cru to the next 50 years **rain** sky falling through the frame **rain** a view from the void new dolphins at Seaworld entertain the crowd ouvrez random movement of the stock .

# Dr Zhivago

It is secondi scivolare in minuti  on the hill opposite<br>
man with a shovel  rhythm of his movements  shovels<br>
the landscape of white white  snow   la neige qui tombe<br>
Lara  Dr Z  this is your white window   skinny  fox<br>
sneaks through the arms of a park  white balloon<br>
daubed with a heart drifts past on Leigh Street    springs<br>
out of reach they practice birth of a stillborn lamb<br>
through  the side of a box   on Welsh hills   sheep are<br>
lost in snow drifts    la neige burials   la polar ice melt<br>
white window landscape   Portia's sheep is stuck in the<br>
dip because once inverted  they're big balls fluff with<br>
feet   white wool caught in a la neve    la neige    Il bianco<br>
della neve al suolo  O Lara Dr Z    skinny fox   la neve<br>
Bianca  nel cielo   snow in the furrows across a field<br>
white lace window   sneeuw op de daken van huizen<br>
in drifts la neige qui tombe    the arctic ice  pack    this<br>
glacier

# Evergreen

It is territorial  anatomies probiotics internal and
external borders of nature   it is living alongside the
stream of wheat    it is evergreen thriving ensconced in
limp winter   something transformative about snow   in
the common lands we are telluric growl   all landscape
commodity scream anti-screen   we witness nomadic
earth we are tuned to soil   we are evergreen blocked
tuned to vast hubs it is survival through ionizing
radiation masts    are interrelated in the two beating
heart in the night of infinite memory    in the schedules
of  seeds    in small breezes through the blocks   it is
looking past autumn's  greyness to the oncoming

# Wanderers

It is  walking DNA moving with the season   voices from
our silent past through sphagnum moss   through layers
discordant   small moon flicker light   nomads in a
monadic universe   sowing and setting bulb song   tree
fronds building greyscapes on a greenwood board
green wanderers slipping through shadow and soil
canadian forests   multinational clear cutting swathes
displace Innuit and Cree  connection with the land
connection with caribou lynx tamarask   bear    wood
bison     moose  falling in rhythm with the woodcutters
inability to empathise with tree green wanderers
slipping through

# Roots.

My father drinks tea talks about his childhood in the
Guyanese rainforest the family's annual upriver surge
to a house on stilts they grew mangoes breadfruit
bananas starfruit yam caught fish rivershrimp
cleaned teeth with a twig from the neem watched
anteater peccary jaguar pad along paths a family
disarticulated a family dispersed India Guyana UK
USA everybody's talking crop colonies trade patterns
disarticulation of family from origin global agriculture
disarticulation of farming from ecosystem laboratory
maverick combined chemical harvesting terminator
seeds a one year GM crop that just stops while the
world's grumbling appendix beats a new climactic jet
silhouettes dip and shallow over earth bees whisper
over once vital soil detectable toxic residues reaching
mouths through fruit vegetables cereals stunting
roots we cannot grow within without.